Favored, Focused, and Fierce
www.edandangelthecooperchronicles.com

My Notes

Date :

Favored, Focused, and Fierce

My Checklist

☐ _____

☐ _____

☐ _____

☐ _____

☐ _____

☐ _____

Favored, Focused, and Fierce

My Notes

Date :

Favored, Focused, and Fierce

My Checklist

Date :

- [ ]
- [ ]
- [ ]
- [ ]
- [ ]
- [ ]

Favored, Focused, and Fierce

www.edandangelthecooperchronicles.com

My Notes

Date :
_____

Favored, Focused, and Fierce
www.edandangelthecooperchronicles.com

My Checklist

Date:

- [ ]
- [ ]
- [ ]
- [ ]
- [ ]
- [ ]

My Notes

Date : _____

_____
_____
_____
_____
_____
_____
_____
_____
_____
_____
_____
_____
_____
_____
_____
_____
_____
_____
_____
_____
_____
_____
_____
_____

My Checklist

Date:

- [ ]
- [ ]
- [ ]
- [ ]
- [ ]
- [ ]

Favored, Focused, and Fierce

My Notes

Date :

_____

_____

_____

_____

_____

_____

_____

_____

_____

_____

_____

_____

_____

_____

_____

_____

_____

_____

_____

_____

_____

_____

_____

My Checklist

Date :

- [ ]
- [ ]
- [ ]
- [ ]
- [ ]
- [ ]

My Notes

Date: _____

_____

_____

_____

_____

_____

_____

_____

_____

_____

_____

_____

_____

_____

_____

_____

_____

_____

_____

_____

_____

_____

_____

_____

_____

_____

_____

_____

_____

Favored, Focused, and Fierce

www.edandangelthecooperchronicles.com

My Checklist

Date :

- [ ]
- [ ]
- [ ]
- [ ]
- [ ]
- [ ]

Favored, Focused, and Fierce

www.edandangelthecooperchronicles.com

My Notes

Date :

_____

_____

_____

_____

_____

_____

_____

_____

_____

_____

_____

_____

_____

_____

_____

_____

_____

_____

_____

_____

_____

_____

_____

My Checklist

Date :

☐

☐

☐

☐

☐

☐

☐

Favored, Focused, and Fierce

www.edandangelthecooperchronicles.com

My Notes

Date :

Favored, Focused, and Fierce

www.edandangelthecooperchronicles.com

My Checklist

Date :

- [ ]
- [ ]
- [ ]
- [ ]
- [ ]
- [ ]

Favored, Focused, and Fierce

www.edandangelthecooperchronicles.com

My Notes

Date :

Favored, Focused, and Fierce
www.edandangelthecooperchronicles.com

My Checklist

Date :

- [ ]
- [ ]
- [ ]
- [ ]
- [ ]
- [ ]

Favored, Focused, and Fierce

www.edandangelthecooperchronicles.com

My Notes

Date :

_____

_____

_____

_____

_____

_____

_____

_____

_____

_____

_____

_____

_____

_____

_____

_____

_____

_____

_____

_____

_____

_____

_____

_____

Favored, Focused, and Fierce
www.edandangelthecooperchronicles.com

My Checklist

Date :

- [ ]
- [ ]
- [ ]
- [ ]
- [ ]
- [ ]

My Notes

Date :

_____

_____

_____

_____

_____

_____

_____

_____

_____

_____

_____

_____

_____

_____

_____

_____

_____

_____

_____

_____

_____

_____

_____

_____

My Checklist

Date:

- [ ]
- [ ]
- [ ]
- [ ]
- [ ]
- [ ]

Favored, Focused, and Fierce

My Notes

Date : _____

_____

_____

_____

_____

_____

_____

_____

_____

_____

_____

_____

_____

_____

_____

_____

_____

_____

_____

_____

_____

_____

_____

Favored, Focused, and Fierce
www.edandangelthecooperchronicles.com

My Checklist

Date :

- [ ]
- [ ]
- [ ]
- [ ]
- [ ]
- [ ]

My Notes

Date :

_____
_____
_____
_____
_____
_____
_____
_____
_____
_____
_____
_____
_____
_____
_____
_____
_____
_____
_____
_____
_____
_____
_____
_____
_____

My Checklist

Date:

- [ ]
- [ ]
- [ ]
- [ ]
- [ ]
- [ ]

Favored, Focused, and Fierce

www.edandangelthecooperchronicles.com

My Notes

Date :

_____

_____

_____

_____

_____

_____

_____

_____

_____

_____

_____

_____

_____

_____

_____

_____

_____

_____

_____

_____

_____

_____

_____

Favored, Focused, and Fierce

My Checklist

☐ _____

☐ _____

☐ _____

☐ _____

☐ _____

☐ _____

Favored, Focused, and Fierce

www.edandangelthecooperchronicles.com

My Notes

Date:

Favored, Focused, and Fierce

My Checklist

Date :

☐

☐

☐

☐

☐

☐

☐

Favored, Focused, and Fierce

www.edandangelthecooperchronicles.com

My Notes

Date :

_____
_____
_____
_____
_____
_____
_____
_____
_____
_____
_____
_____
_____
_____
_____
_____
_____
_____
_____
_____
_____
_____
_____
_____
_____
_____

My Checklist

☐

☐

☐

☐

☐

☐

Favored, Focused, and Fierce

My Notes

Date:

_____

My Checklist

- [ ]
- [ ]
- [ ]
- [ ]
- [ ]
- [ ]

Favored, Focused, and Fierce

www.edandangelthecooperchronicles.com

My Notes

Date :

_____

_____
_____
_____
_____
_____
_____
_____
_____
_____
_____
_____
_____
_____
_____
_____
_____
_____
_____
_____
_____
_____
_____
_____
_____
_____

My Checklist

Date :

- [ ]
- [ ]
- [ ]
- [ ]
- [ ]
- [ ]

My Notes

Date :

_____

_____

_____

_____

_____

_____

_____

_____

_____

_____

_____

_____

_____

_____

_____

_____

_____

_____

_____

_____

_____

_____

Favored, Focused, and Fierce

My Checklist

☐ _____

☐ _____

☐ _____

☐ _____

☐ _____

☐ _____

Favored, Focused, and Fierce

My Notes

Date :

_____
_____
_____
_____
_____
_____
_____
_____
_____
_____
_____
_____
_____
_____
_____
_____
_____
_____
_____
_____
_____
_____
_____

Favored, Focused, and Fierce
www.edandangelthecooperchronicles.com

My Checklist

Date :

- [ ]
- [ ]
- [ ]
- [ ]
- [ ]
- [ ]

Favored, Focused, and Fierce

My Notes

Date :

_____

_____

_____

_____

_____

_____

_____

_____

_____

_____

_____

_____

_____

_____

_____

_____

_____

_____

_____

_____

_____

_____

_____

_____

Favored, Focused, and Fierce

My Checklist

Date :

- [ ]
- [ ]
- [ ]
- [ ]
- [ ]
- [ ]

Favored, Focused, and Fierce

www.edandangelthecooperchronicles.com

My Notes

Date : _____

_____
_____
_____
_____
_____
_____
_____
_____
_____
_____
_____
_____
_____
_____
_____
_____
_____
_____
_____
_____
_____
_____
_____
_____
_____
_____

My Checklist

Date :

- [ ]
- [ ]
- [ ]
- [ ]
- [ ]
- [ ]

Favored, Focused, and Fierce

www.edandangelthecooperchronicles.com

My Schedule

Sunday :	Thursday:
Monday :	Friday :
Tuesday :	Saturday :
Wednesday :	*Notes* :

MySchedule

Sunday :	Thursday:

Monday :	Friday :

Tuesday :	Saturday :

Wednesday :	Notes :

MySchedule

Sunday :	Thursday :
Monday :	Friday :
Tuesday :	Saturday :
Wednesday :	*Notes* :

MySchedule

Sunday :	Thursday :

Monday :	Friday :

Tuesday :	Saturday :

Wednesday :	Notes :

Thank you for your purchase.

Don't forget to get your copy of "Favored, Focused, and Fierce" by Angel Cooper. Also, get your copy of "Love is Worth the Work" by Ed and Angel Cooper. Available on Amazon.

Favored, Focused, and Fierce
www.edandangelthecooperchronicles.com

Made in the USA
Columbia, SC
09 November 2021